Features

These Skills Are Presented in Various Ways Throughout *3-2-1 Learn* for Ages 2–3
- Traces lines, shapes, numbers, and letter formations
- Counts objects
- Uses positional words such as *on*, *off*, *in*, *out*
- Compares sizes, shapes, and quantities
- Sorts and classifies objects
- Matches letters
- Names basic colors
- Names body parts
- Identifies some letters
- Retells information
- Sings rhymes and songs

ACTIVITIES IN THIS BOOK ARE PRESENTED BY THE SUBJECT AREAS OF LANGUAGE ARTS, MATH, SCIENCE, AND SOCIAL STUDIES.

Pages in the Language Arts Section Provide:
- Tracing letter formations
- Naming letters of the alphabet
- Practice holding writing tools correctly
- Making letter-sound associations

Pages in the Math Section Provide:
- Naming shapes
- Naming and writing numbers
- Counting
- Positional words
- Classifying

3-2-1 Learn, SV 9781419099267

Pages in the Science Section Introduce Concepts:

- Plants and Animals Grow and Change
- Plants and Animals Have Basic Needs
- Our Bodies Need Good Care
- Our Five Senses Help Us Observe
  the World Around Us

Pages in the Social Studies Section Introduce Concepts:

- People Need Shelter
- Families Are Different
- Families Observe Traditions and Celebrations
- People Have Jobs
- Money Buys Things
- Transportation Helps People

Features
3-2-1 Learn, SV 9781419099267

Stages of Development

STAGES OF DEVELOPMENT OF TWO- AND THREE-YEAR-OLDS

The intellectual development of a two-year-old is simple and concrete. This stage opens the door for the three-year-old and a broader range of skills. Because each child is unique and learns at his or her own pace, it is important for parents to follow their child's lead in determining when to introduce various skills.

A two-year-old

- enjoys simple stories
- uses 2-word or 3-word sentences
- says names of toys
- enjoys looking at books
- knows 5 to 6 body parts
- repeats words
- is interested in learning how to use common objects
- repeats simple songs and rhymes
- knows name
- makes straight and curved strokes
- knows some numbers
- understands the concepts of *1* and *2*
- matches object to picture
- understands *in*, *out*, *over*, *under*
- matches circles and squares

A three-year-old

- talks in complete sentences of 3 to 5 words
- enjoys repeating words and sounds
- listens attentively to short stories and books
- repeats simple rhymes and songs
- tells simple stories from pictures or books
- asks *who*, *what*, *where*, and *why* questions
- draws a circle and square
- matches objects to pictures
- identifies common colors
- can count 4 to 5 objects
- understands concepts up to *4* or *5*
- can solve simple, concrete problems
- identifies similarities and differences
- is interested in features of animals that make them unique
- identifies some letters
- writes with lines and scribbles
- understands position words

STANDARDS

The standards listed below are repeated throughout the book. It is important to keep in mind that young children develop at different rates. Some children will be taking the first steps toward understanding the concepts, while others will be mastering them. The standards can be used with your child to guide practice and to measure progress.

Language Arts

Begins to recognize and name some letters
Begins to understand that letters make sounds
Begins to use a pencil or crayons effectively
Begins to name basic colors
Retells information
Participates in song and rhymes

Math

Uses positional terms to describe relationships
   among objects
Begins to sort and classify objects by one attribute
Begins to draw common shapes
Begins to compare shapes
Begins to understand concepts of *more than*,
   less than, and *equal*
Counts objects using one-to-one correspondence
Demonstrates a beginning understanding of measurement
Begins to name basic geometric shapes
Makes comparisons using the terms *same* and *different*

Science

Begins to understand about how living things function, adapt, and change
Uses senses to explore and observe materials
Names major body parts
Begins to make comparisons among objects that have been observed
Begins to describe basic needs of living things, such as air and water

Social Studies

Understands that humans need clothing and shelter
Begins to identify differences among people
Begins to identify differences among families
Begins to understand family customs and traditions
Begins to understand concept of location
Begins to use terms that tell locations such as *near, far, left,* and *right*
Begins to identify jobs that people do
Begins to understand why people have jobs
Identifies the United States flag

Standards
3-2-1 Learn, SV 9781419099267

Left to Right

Directions: Have your child follow the broken lines from left to right with a finger. Then encourage your child to use a jumbo crayon or pencil to trace the lines. Invite your child to color the pictures.

3-2-1 Learn, SV 9781419099267

Top to Bottom

Directions: Have your child follow the broken lines from top to bottom with a finger. Then encourage your child to use a jumbo crayon or pencil to trace the lines. Invite your child to color the pictures.

3-2-1 Learn, SV 9781419099267

T Is for Tree

Directions: Name the object and the letter. Invite your child to put a finger on the starting point to "write" the letter. Then encourage your child to use a jumbo crayon or pencil to trace the letter again. Have your child color the picture.

Letter *T*
3-2-1 Learn, SV 9781419099267

<u>L</u> Is for Lion

Directions: Name the object and the letter. Invite your child to put a finger on the starting point to "write" the letter. Then encourage your child to use a jumbo crayon or pencil to trace the letter. Have your child color the picture.

Letter *L*
3-2-1 Learn, SV 9781419099267

H Is for Hat

Directions: Name the object and the letter. Invite your child to put a finger on the starting point to "write" the letter. Then encourage your child to use a jumbo crayon or pencil to trace the letter. Have your child color the picture.

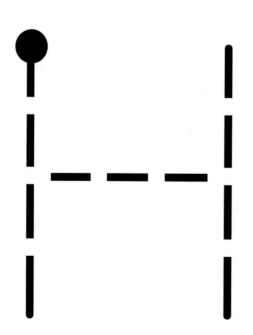

Letter _H_
3-2-1 Learn, SV 9781419099267

<u>E</u> Is for Egg

Directions: Name the object and the letter. Invite your child to put a finger on the starting point to "write" the letter. Then encourage your child to use a jumbo crayon or pencil to trace the letter. Have your child color the picture.

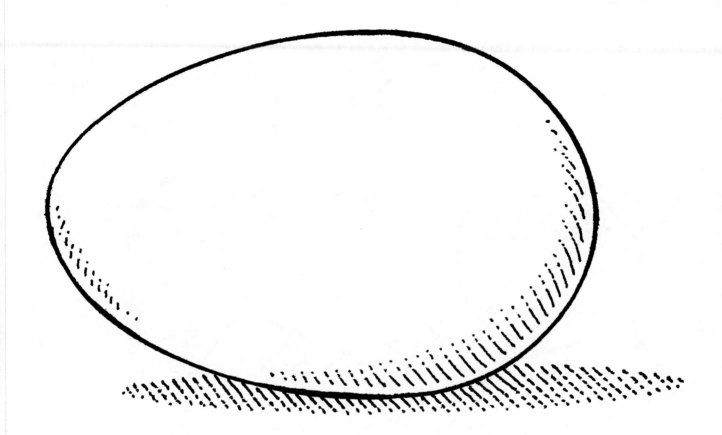

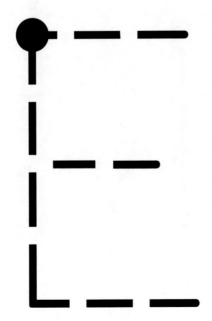

F Is for Fish

Directions: Name the object and the letter. Invite your child to put a finger on the starting point to "write" the letter. Then encourage your child to use a jumbo crayon or pencil to trace the letter. Have your child color the picture.

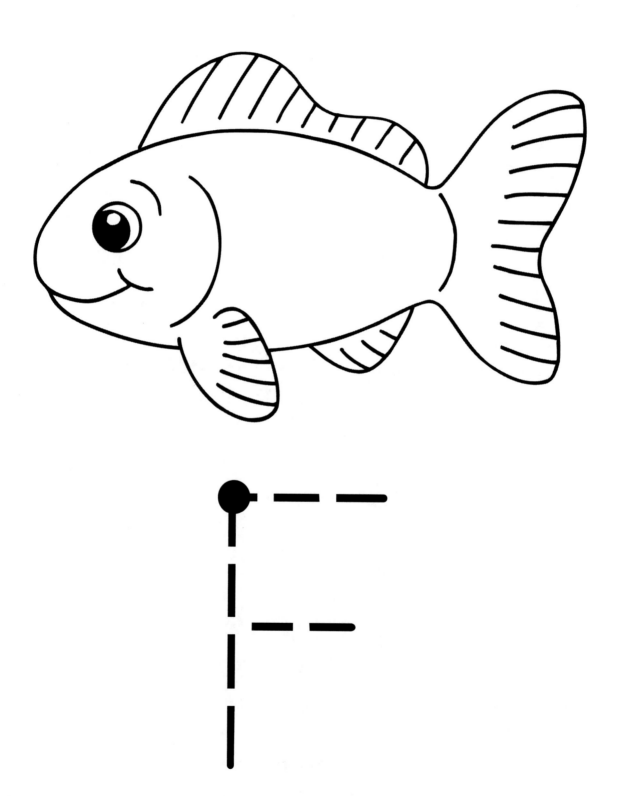

12

Letter F
3-2-1 Learn, SV 9781419099267

I Is for Igloo

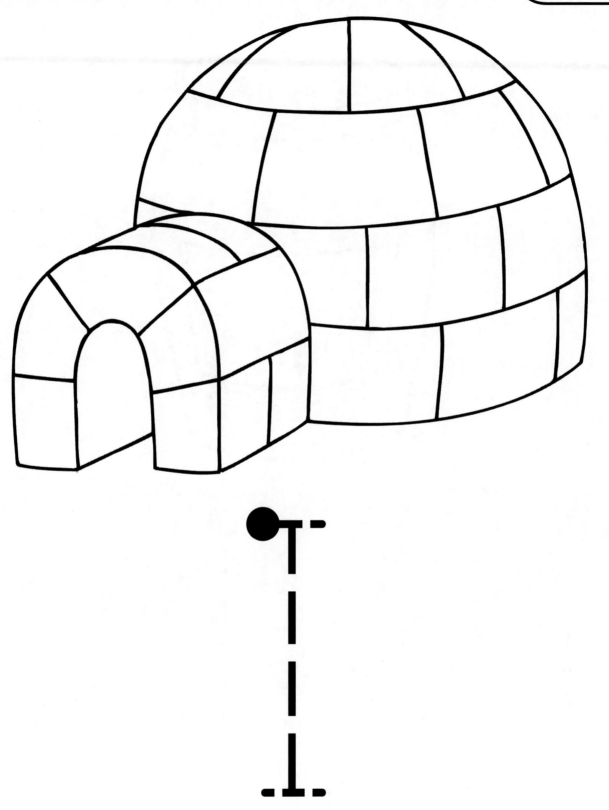

3-2-1 Learn, SV 9781419099267

J Is for Jar

Directions: Name the object and the letter. Invite your child to put a finger on the starting point to "write" the letter. Then encourage your child to use a jumbo crayon or pencil to trace the letter again. Have your child color the picture.

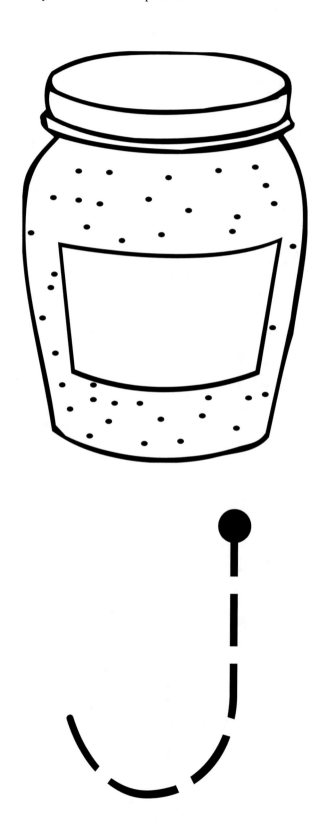

3-2-1 Learn, SV 9781419099267

Diagonal Lines

Directions: Have your child follow the broken diagonal lines from top to bottom with a finger. Then encourage your child to use a jumbo crayon or pencil to trace the lines. Have your child color the picture.

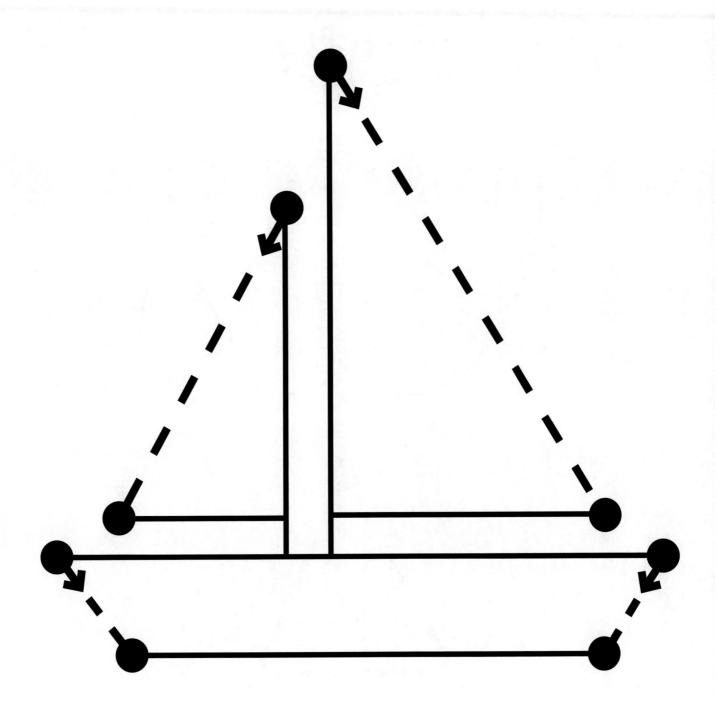

Trace Diagonal Lines
3-2-1 Learn, SV 9781419099267

<u>A</u> Is for Apple

Directions: Name the object and the letter. Invite your child to put a finger on the starting point to "write" the letter. Then encourage your child to use a jumbo crayon or pencil to trace the letter. Have your child color the picture.

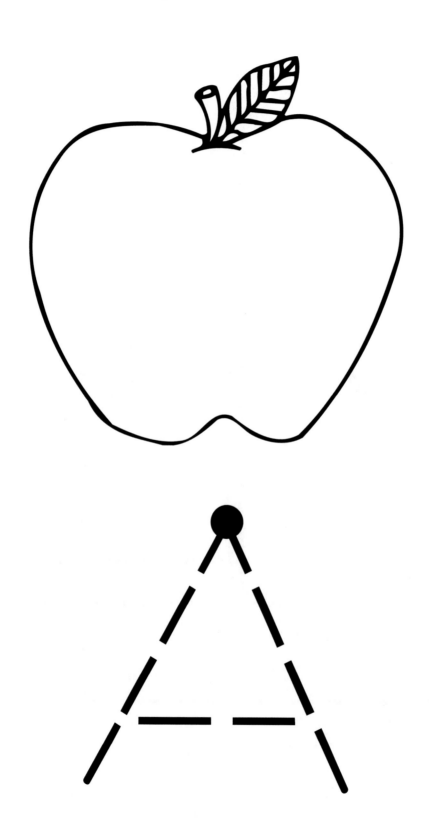

X Is for X-ray

V Is for Vest

Directions: Name the object and the letter. Invite your child to put a finger on the starting point to "write" the letter. Then encourage your child to use a jumbo crayon or pencil to trace the letter. Have your child color the picture.

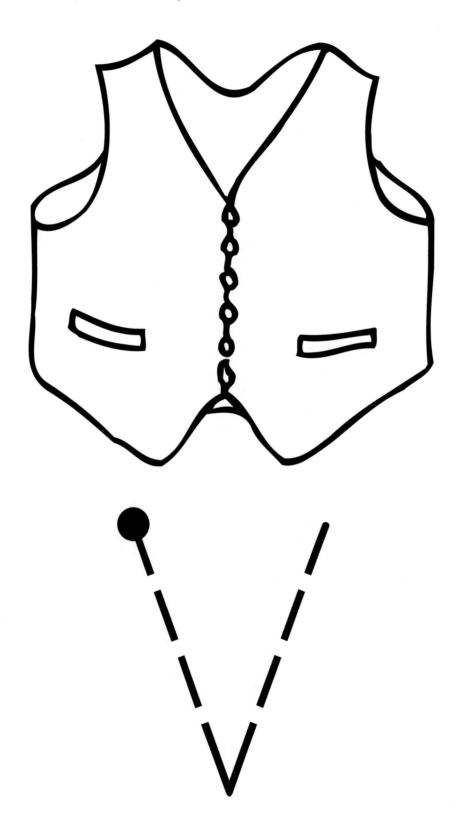

3-2-1 Learn, SV 9781419099267

W Is for Wagon

Directions: Name the object and the letter. Invite your child to put a finger on the starting point to "write" the letter. Then encourage your child to use a jumbo crayon or pencil to trace the letter. Have your child color the picture.

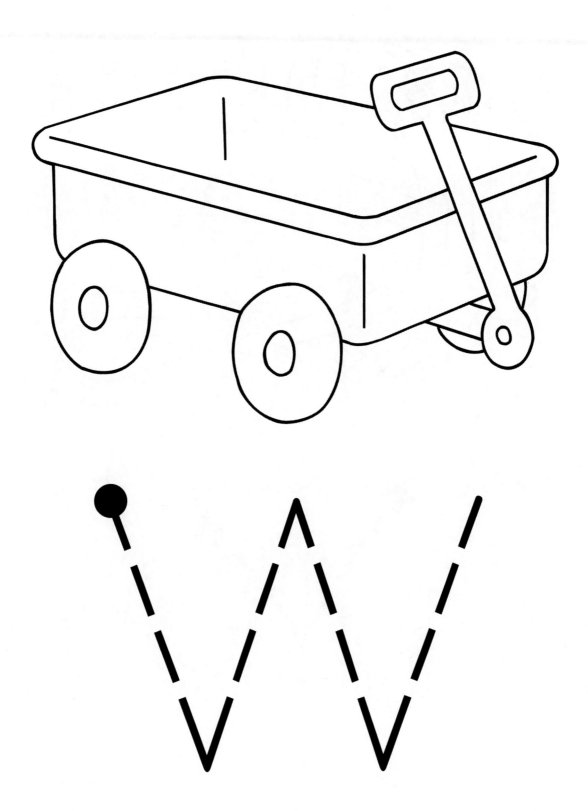

Letter W
3-2-1 Learn, SV 9781419099267

Y Is for Yarn

Directions: Name the object and the letter. Invite your child to put a finger on the starting point to "write" the letter. Then encourage your child to use a jumbo crayon or pencil to trace the letter. Have your child color the picture.

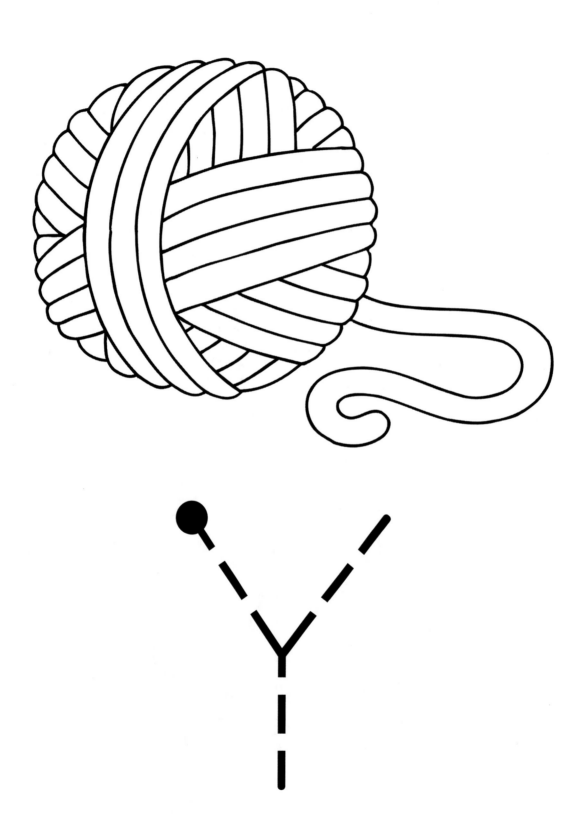

3-2-1 Learn, SV 9781419099267

<u>M</u> Is for Mittens

Directions: Name the object and the letter. Invite your child to put a finger on the starting point to "write" the letter. Then encourage your child to use a jumbo crayon or pencil to trace the letter. Have your child color the picture.

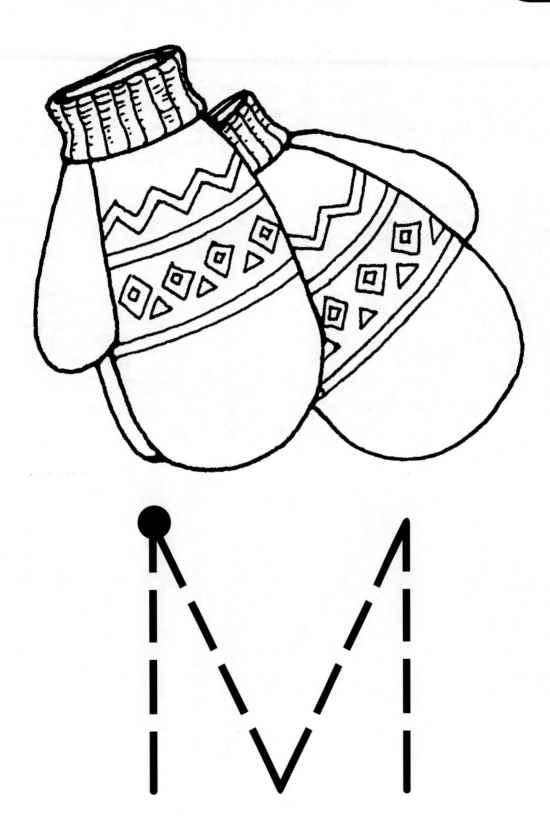

Letter *M*
3-2-1 Learn, SV 9781419099267

N Is for Nest

Directions: Name the object and the letter. Invite your child to put a finger on the starting point to "write" the letter. Then encourage your child to use a jumbo crayon or pencil to trace the letter. Have your child color the picture.

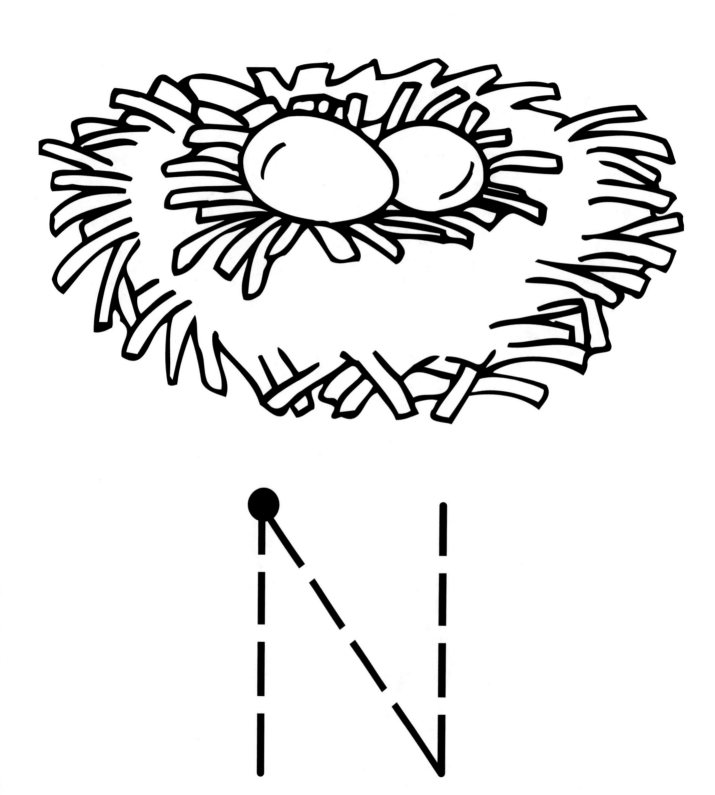

3-2-1 Learn, SV 9781419099267

<u>K</u> Is for Key

Directions: Name the object and the letter. Invite your child to put a finger on the starting point to "write" the letter. Then encourage your child to use a jumbo crayon or pencil to trace the letter. Have your child color the picture.

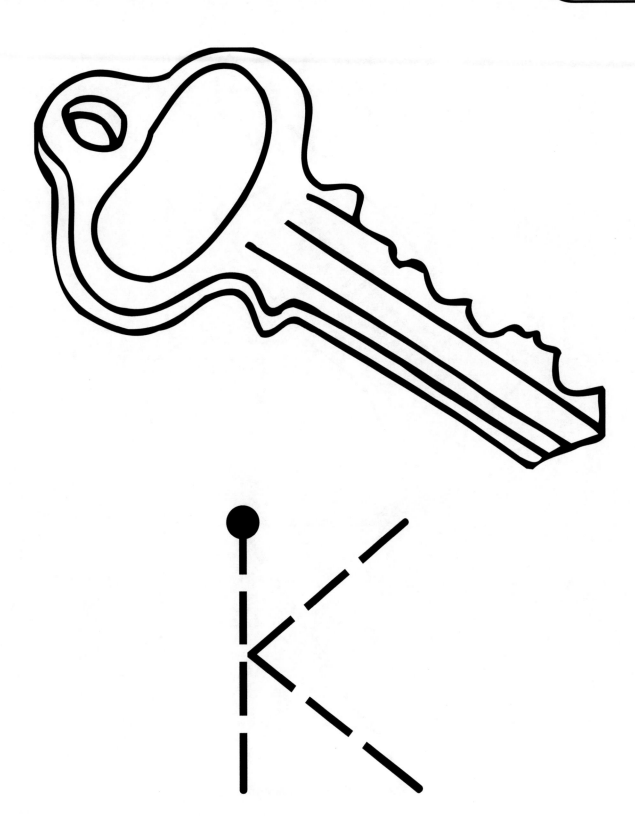

3-2-1 Learn, SV 9781419099267

Z Is for Zipper

Directions: Name the object and the letter. Invite your child to put a finger on the starting point to "write" the letter. Then encourage your child to use a jumbo crayon or pencil to trace the letter. Have your child color the picture.

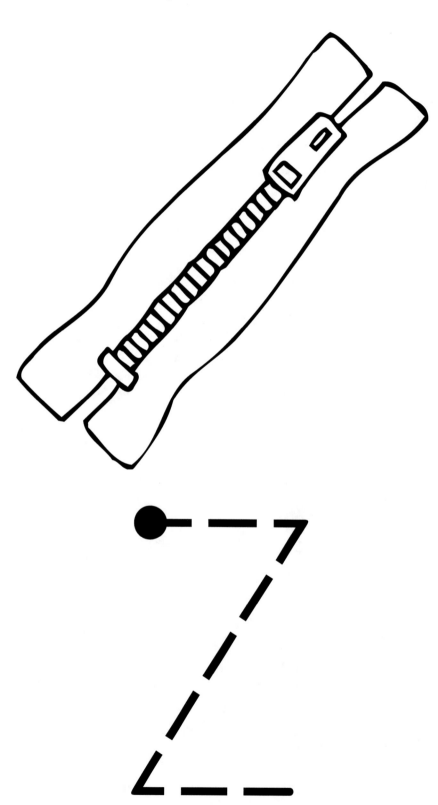

Letter Z
3-2-1 Learn, SV 9781419099267

A Right Curve

Directions: Have your child follow the broken curved line from top to bottom with a finger. Then encourage your child to use a jumbo crayon or pencil to trace the line. Invite your child to color the picture.

Trace Right Half Circles
3-2-1 Learn, SV 9781419099267

<u>D</u> Is for Doll

Directions: Name the object and the letter. Invite your child to put a finger on the starting point to "write" the letter. Then encourage your child to use a jumbo crayon or pencil to trace the letter. Have your child color the picture.

3-2-1 Learn, SV 9781419099267

P Is for Pencil

Directions: Name the object and the letter. Invite your child to put a finger on the starting point to "write" the letter. Then encourage your child to use a jumbo crayon or pencil to trace the letter. Have your child color the picture.

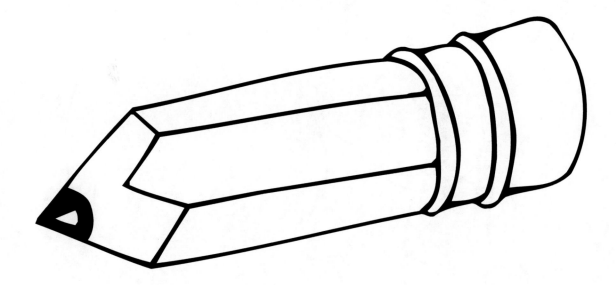

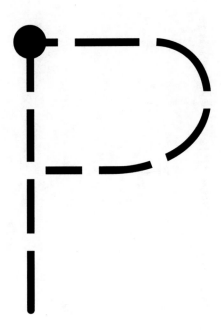

Letter *P*
3-2-1 Learn, SV 9781419099267

<u>B</u> Is for Bear

Directions: Name the object and the letter. Invite your child to put a finger on the starting point to "write" the letter. Then encourage your child to use a jumbo crayon or pencil to trace the letter. Have your child color the picture.

Letter *B*
3-2-1 Learn, SV 9781419099267

<u>R</u> Is for Rabbit

Directions: Name the object and the letter. Invite your child to put a finger on the starting point to "write" the letter. Then encourage your child to use a jumbo crayon or pencil to trace the letter. Have your child color the picture.

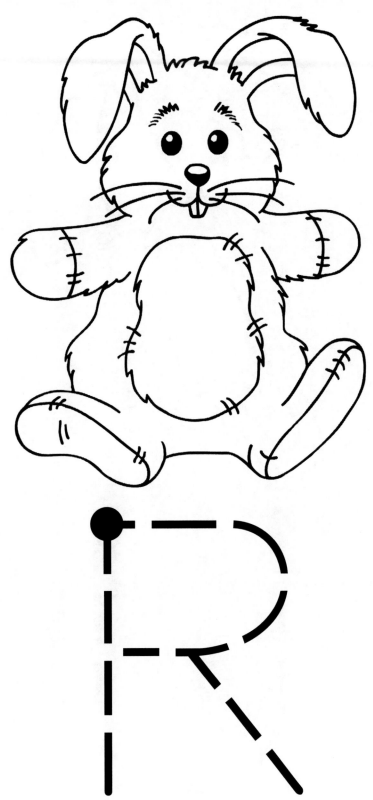

Letter *R*
3-2-1 Learn, SV 9781419099267

<u>U</u> Is for Umbrella

Directions: Name the object and the letter. Invite your child to put a finger on the starting point to "write" the letter. Then encourage your child to use a jumbo crayon or pencil to trace the letter. Have your child color the picture.

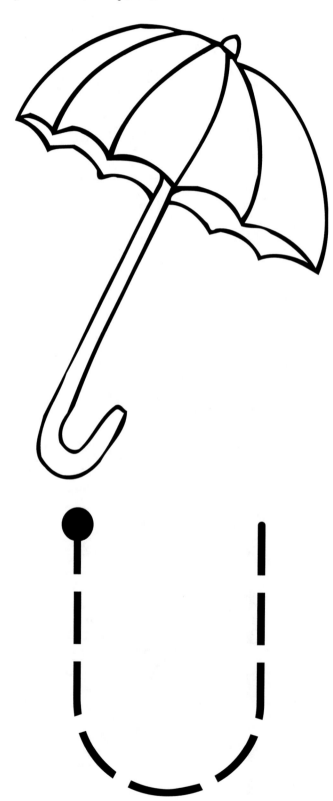

3-2-1 Learn, SV 9781419099267

A Left Curve

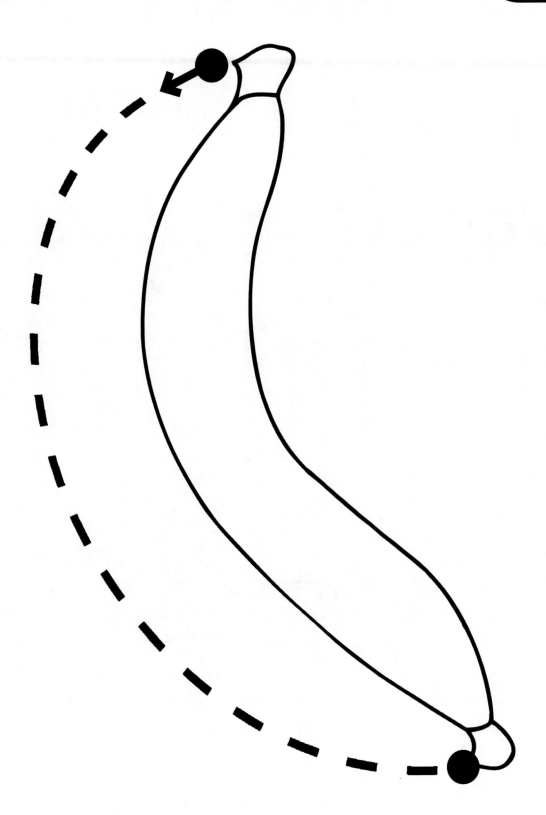

Trace Left Half Circles
3-2-1 Learn, SV 9781419099267

Flying in Circles

Directions: Have your child follow the broken lines on the circles with a finger. Then encourage your child to use a jumbo crayon or pencil to trace the circles to finish the picture. Invite your child to color the picture.

<u>C</u> Is for Cat

Directions: Name the object and the letter. Invite your child to put a finger on the starting point to "write" the letter. Then encourage your child to use a jumbo crayon or pencil to trace the letter. Have your child color the picture.

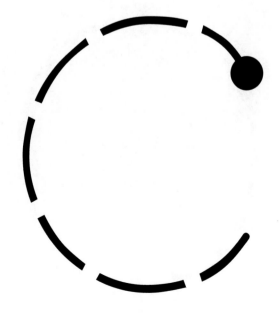

3-2-1 Learn, SV 9781419099267

O Is for Octopus

Directions: Name the object and the letter. Invite your child to put a finger on the starting point to "write" the letter. Then encourage your child to use a jumbo crayon or pencil to trace the letter. Have your child color the picture.

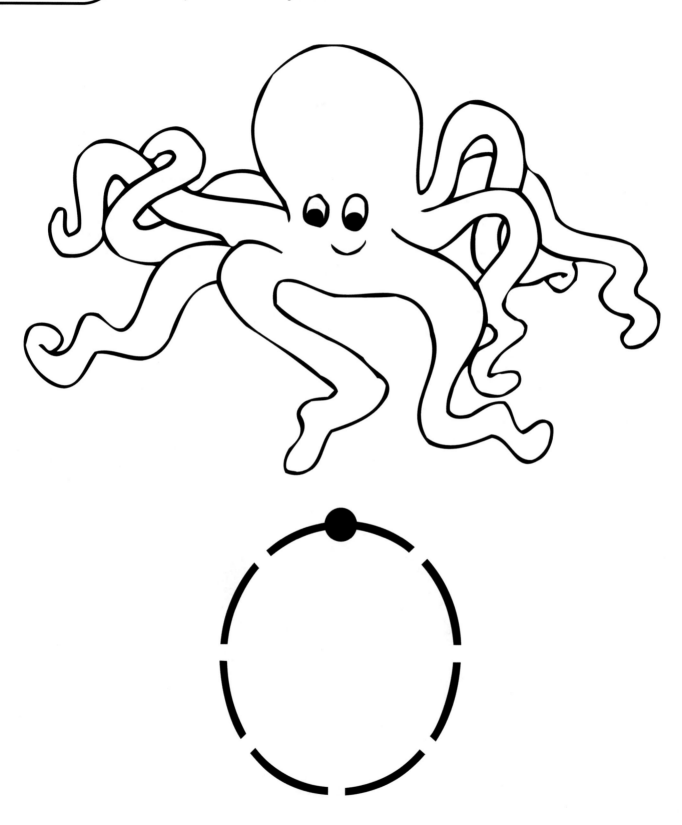

Letter *O*
3-2-1 Learn, SV 9781419099267

G Is for Grapes

Directions: Name the object and the letter. Invite your child to put a finger on the starting point to "write" the letter. Then encourage your child to use a jumbo crayon or pencil to trace the letter. Have your child color the picture.

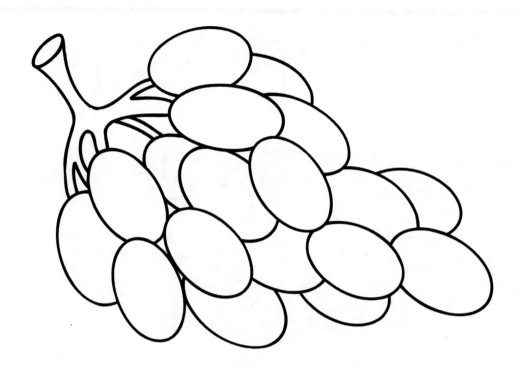

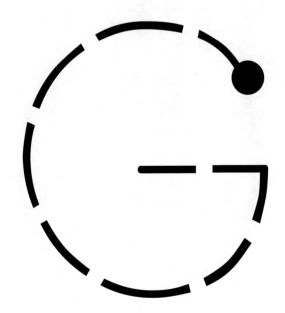

Letter G
3-2-1 Learn, SV 9781419099267

Q Is for Quilt

Directions: Name the object and the letter. Invite your child to put a finger on the starting point to "write" the letter. Then encourage your child to use a jumbo crayon or pencil to trace the letter. Have your child color the picture.

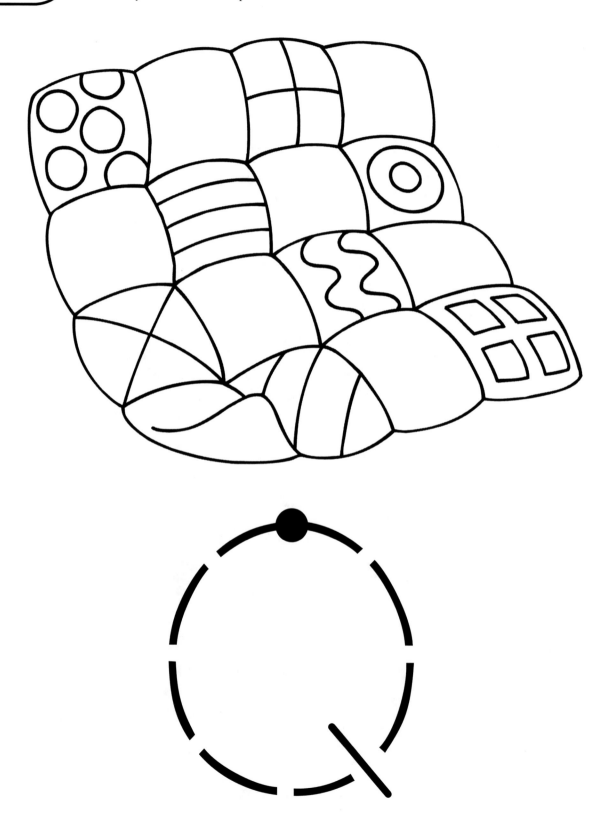

3-2-1 Learn, SV 9781419099267

<u>S</u> Is for Sun

Directions: Name the object and the letter. Invite your child to put a finger on the starting point to "write" the letter. Then encourage your child to use a jumbo crayon or pencil to trace the letter. Have your child color the picture.

Letter S
3-2-1 Learn, SV 9781419099267

Circles

Directions: Have your child color all of the circles.

Circles
3-2-1 Learn, SV 9781419099267

Squares

Directions: Have your child color all of the squares.

39

Squares
3-2-1 Learn, SV 9781419099267

Rectangles

Directions: Have your child color all of the rectangles.

3-2-1 Learn, SV 9781419099267

Triangles

Directions: Have your child color all of the triangles.

Shapes

Directions: Have your child use a purple crayon to color the biggest shape in each row, an orange crayon to color the medium-sized shape, and a green crayon to color the littlest shape.

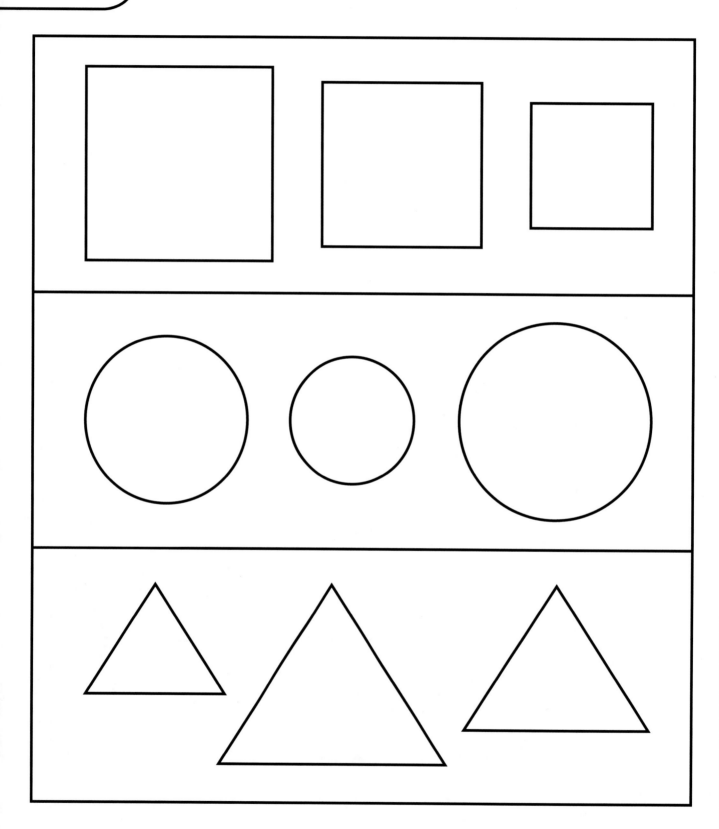

Big and Little Shapes
3-2-1 Learn, SV 9781419099267

A Shape Butterfly

Directions: Have your child count each shape in the butterfly and tell which shape appears the most number of times. Then have your child color the picture.

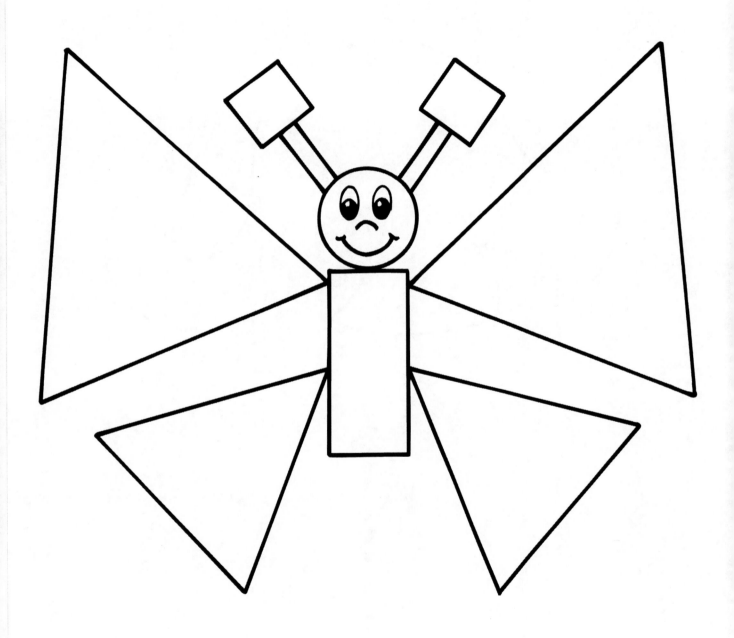

Count Shapes
3-2-1 Learn, SV 9781419099267

Number 1

3-2-1 Learn, SV 9781419099267

Number 2

Directions: Have your child count the stars and use a jumbo crayon or pencil to trace the number. Then have your child pick a yellow crayon from the crayon box and color the stars.

Number 2
3-2-1 Learn, SV 9781419099267

Number 3

Directions: Have your child count the birds and use a jumbo crayon or pencil to trace the number. Then have your child pick a blue crayon from the crayon box and color the birds.

3-2-1 Learn, SV 9781419099267

Number 4

Directions: Have your child count the leaves and use a jumbo crayon or pencil to trace the number. Then have your child pick a green crayon from the crayon box and color the leaves.

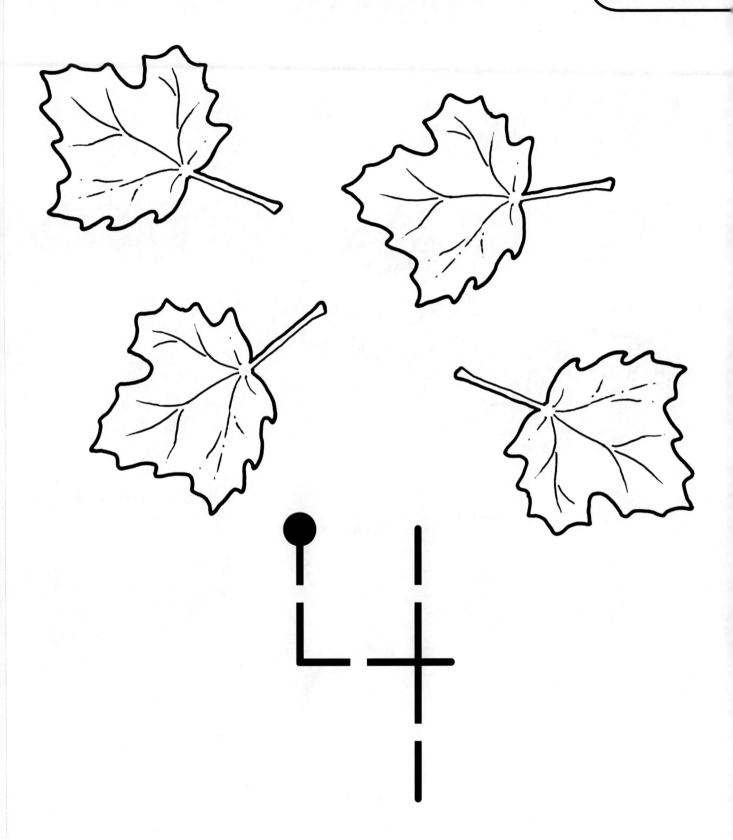

Number 5

Directions: Have your child count the bunches of grapes and use a jumbo crayon or pencil to trace the number. Then have your child pick a purple crayon from the crayon box and color the grapes.

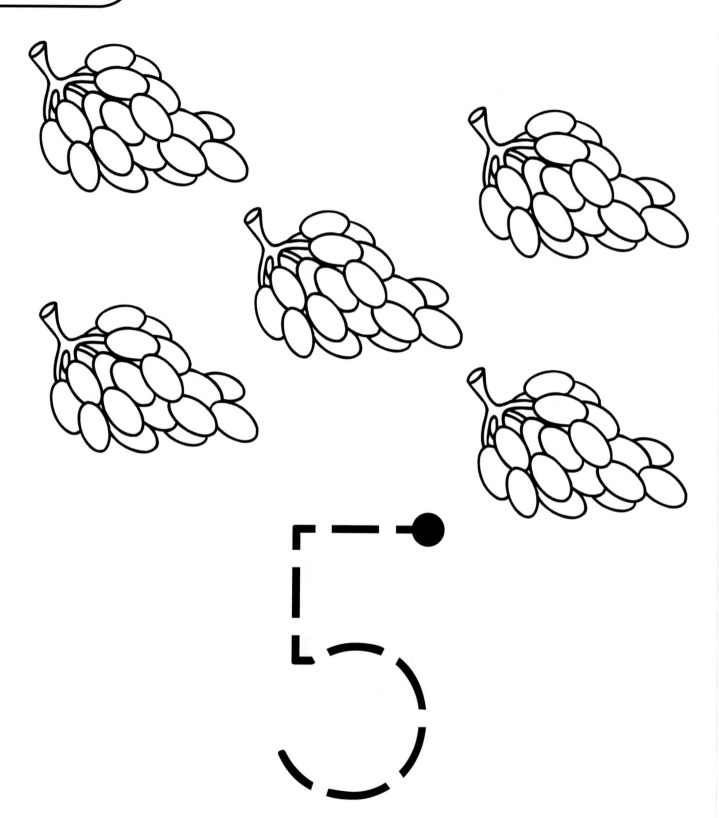

3-2-1 Learn, SV 9781419099267

Number 6

Directions: Have your child count the fish and use a jumbo crayon or pencil to trace the number. Then have your child pick an orange crayon from the crayon box and color the fish.

Number 6
3-2-1 Learn, SV 9781419099267

Number 7

Directions: Have your child count the bugs and use a jumbo crayon or pencil to trace the number. Then have your child pick a black crayon from the crayon box and color the bugs.

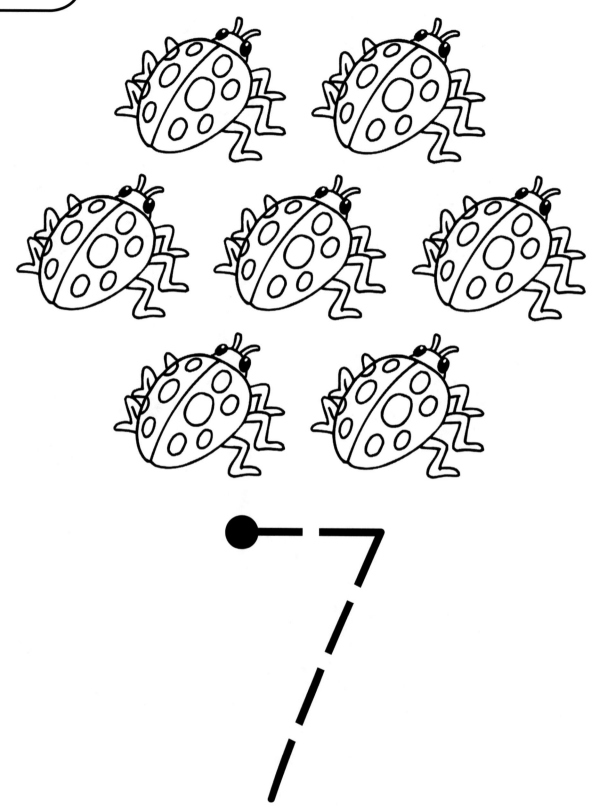

3-2-1 Learn, SV 9781419099267

Number 8

Directions: Have your child count the gingerbread men and use a jumbo crayon or pencil to trace the number. Then have your child pick a brown crayon from the crayon box and color the gingerbread men.

Number *8*
3-2-1 Learn, SV 9781419099267

Number 9

Directions: Have your child count the mice and use a jumbo crayon or pencil to trace the number. Then have your child pick a gray crayon from the crayon box and color the mice.

3-2-1 Learn, SV 9781419099267

Number 10

Directions: Have your child count the flowers and use a jumbo crayon or pencil to trace the number. Then have your child pick a pink crayon from the crayon box and color the flowers.

3-2-1 Learn, SV 9781419099267

Groups of 1

Directions: Have your child count the objects in each box and color the groups that have one object.

3-2-1 Learn, SV 9781419099267

Groups of 2

Directions: Have your child count the objects in each box and color the groups that have two objects.

Groups of 2
3-2-1 Learn, SV 9781419099267

Groups of 3

Directions: Have your child count the objects in each box and color the groups that have three objects.

3-2-1 Learn, SV 9781419099267

Groups of 4

Directions: Have your child count the objects in each box and color the groups that have four objects.

Groups of 5

Directions: Have your child count the objects in each box and color the groups that have five objects.

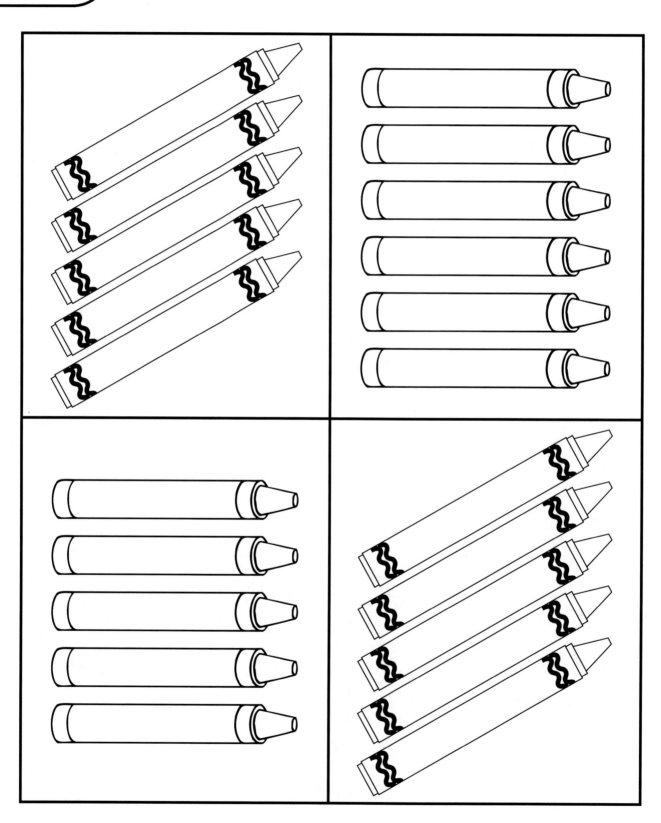

Groups of 5
3-2-1 Learn, SV 9781419099267

Groups of 6

Directions: Have your child count the objects in each box and color the group that has six objects.

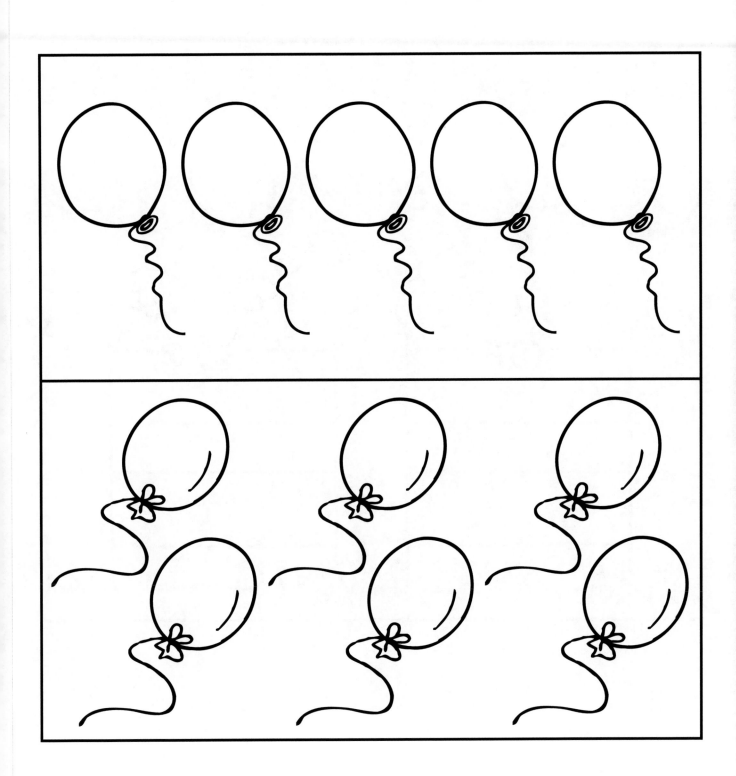

Groups of 6
3-2-1 Learn, SV 9781419099267

On the Fence

Directions: Demonstrate the concept of *on* by placing several items on a table. Have your child color the birds that are *on* the fence.

Birds on the Fence
3-2-1 Learn, SV 9781419099267

Crawling off the Web

Directions: Demonstrate the concept of *off* by taking several books off of a shelf. Have your child color the spider that has crawled *off* the web.

In the Box

Directions: Demonstrate the concept of *in* by putting clothes in a laundry basket. Have your child color the toys that are *in* the toy box.

Toys in a Box
3-2-1 Learn, SV 9781419099267

A Dog Is Out

Directions: Demonstrate the concept of *out* by taking a pair of socks out of the drawer. Have your child color the dog that is *out* of the doghouse.

The Top Shelf

Directions: Demonstrate the concept of the *top* by placing a bowl on top of the refrigerator. Have your child color the books that are on the *top* shelf of the bookcase.

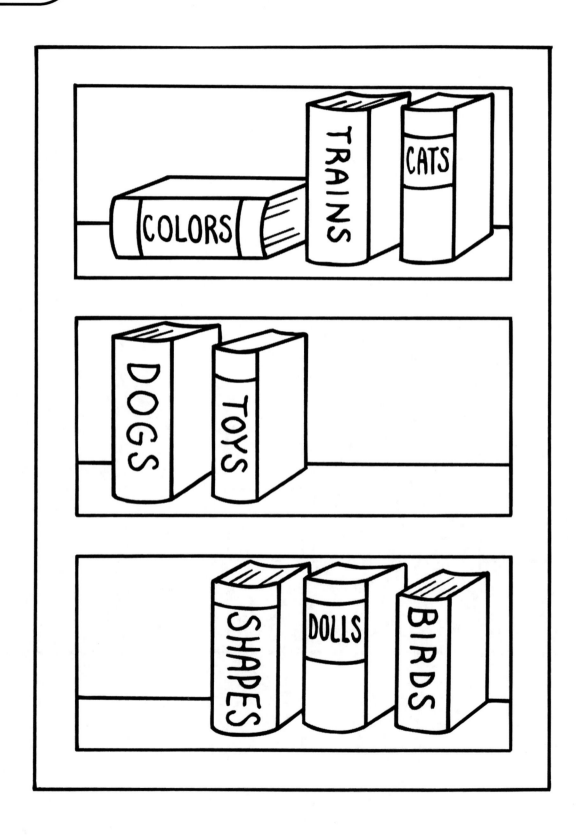

3-2-1 Learn, SV 9781419099267

At the Bottom

Directions: Demonstrate the concept of the *bottom* by opening the bottom drawer of a dresser. Have your child color the fish that is at the *bottom* of the fishbowl.

Fish at the Bottom
3-2-1 Learn, SV 9781419099267

Big Things

Directions: Invite your child to compare furniture in the house that varies in size, such as big tables and little tables or a big bed and a little bed. Then have your child color the things in each row that are big.

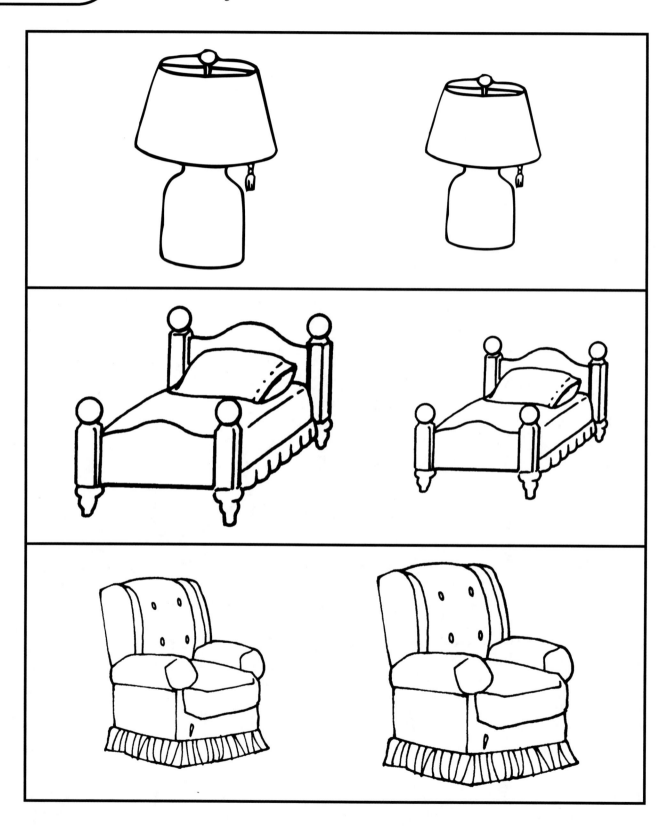

Find Big Things
3-2-1 Learn, SV 9781419099267

Little Things

Directions: Invite your child to compare foods that are little portions or large portions, such as a little muffin and a large muffin or a little pear and a large pear. Then have your child color the things in each row that are little.

Find Little Things
3-2-1 Learn, SV 9781419099267

Find the Same Size

Directions: Have your child look at familiar objects, such as shoes. Point out that two things can be the same size. Then have your child circle the pictures in each row that are the same size.

Biggest and Smallest

Directions: Read the story of *The Three Bears* aloud to your child and point out the things in the story that are different sizes. Then have your child use a green crayon to color the biggest thing in each row and a blue crayon to color the smallest thing in each row.

Compare Biggest and Smallest
3-2-1 Learn, SV 9781419099267

Color the Toys

Directions: Have your child name all of the objects and color the ones that are toys.

Color the Animals

Directions: Have your child name all of the objects and color the ones that are animals.

Classify Animals
3-2-1 Learn, SV 9781419099267

Color the Clothes

Directions: Have your child name all of the objects and color the ones that are clothes.

Classify Clothes
3-2-1 Learn, SV 9781419099267

Color the Foods

Directions: Have your child name all of the objects and color the ones that are foods.

Classify Foods
3-2-1 Learn, SV 9781419099267

An Apple Tree

Directions: Show your child an apple. Read a book to your child about how apples grow on trees. Invite your child to use a jumbo crayon or pencil to trace the apples on the tree. Then have your child color the picture.

Round Apples
3-2-1 Learn, SV 9781419099267

Big Apple, Little Apple

Directions: Show your child a red apple and a green apple. Encourage your child to tell how the apples are different, such as the color or size. Invite your child to color the big apple red and the little apple green.

Big and Little Apples
3-2-1 Learn, SV 9781419099267

Look Alike Leaves

Directions: Go for a walk with your child and look for leaves. Show your child that the leaves on one tree are different from the leaves on another tree. Then have your child use a green crayon to color the leaves below that are the same. Invite your child to use a brown crayon to color the leaf that is different.

Same or Different Leaves
3-2-1 Learn, SV 9781419099267

Which Has More?

Directions: Collect four or five small leaves. Hold two leaves in one hand and one leaf in the other hand. Have your child point to the hand that is holding more leaves. Then invite your child to color the leaves in the box that has more.

More Leaves
3-2-1 Learn, SV 9781419099267

Colorful Vegetables

Directions: Invite your child to look at the vegetables in the produce aisle at the grocery store and name the colors of the vegetables. Then have your child color the vegetables that are orange.

Color the Vegetables
3-2-1 Learn, SV 9781419099267

Plant the Seeds

Directions: Talk to your child about the things a seed needs to grow, such as air, light, water, and soil. Help your child plant a few lima bean seeds in a plastic cup. Provide the seeds with water and light and observe them as they sprout. Have your child count the seeds and color the picture.

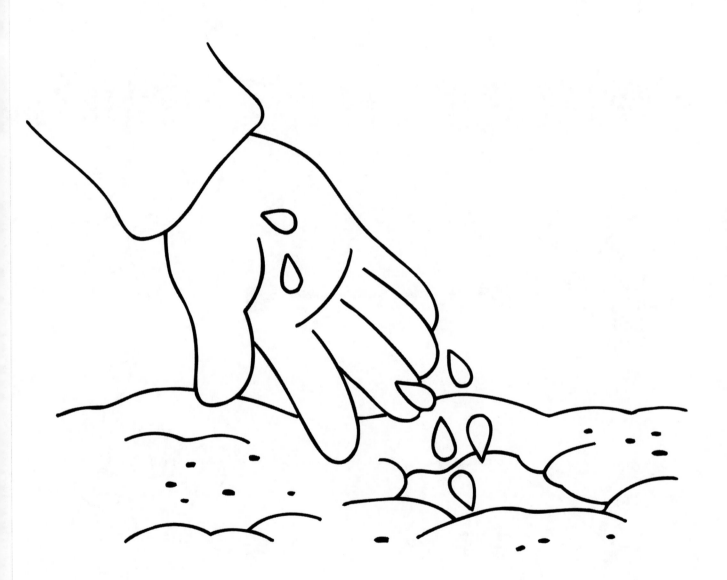

Count Seeds
3-2-1 Learn, SV 9781419099267

Bees and Flowers

Directions: Invite your child to look closely at the pollen inside a flower. Tell your child that bees collect pollen to make honey. Have your child use a jumbo pencil or crayon to trace the lines from left to right.

Trace a Bee's Path
3-2-1 Learn, SV 9781419099267

Ladybugs on Leaves

Directions: Show your child pictures of ladybugs and talk about how ladybugs find their food on leaves. Have your child count the ladybugs on each leaf and draw a circle around the leaf that has more ladybugs.

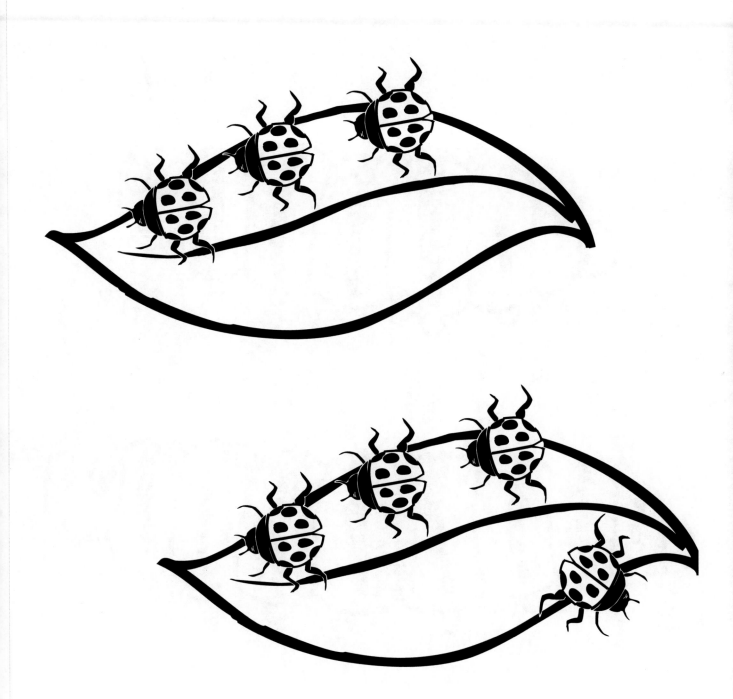

3-2-1 Learn, SV 9781419099267

Lengthy Caterpillars

Directions: Read a book about caterpillars to your child, such as *The Very Hungry Caterpillar* by Eric Carle. Explain that a caterpillar gets longer as it grows. Have your child color the short caterpillar yellow and the long caterpillar green.

Heads Up Turtle

Directions: Have your child name his or her body parts, such as head, arms, and legs. Then have your child tell what body part is missing on the turtle. Encourage your child to draw the turtle's head and color the turtle.

What's Missing on the Turtle?
3-2-1 Learn, SV 9781419099267

A Shapely Turtle

Directions: Show your child a picture of a real turtle. Talk about how the turtle uses its shell for protection. Then have your child look at the turtle below and name the shapes on the turtle's shell. Invite your child to use a green crayon to color the square.

Shapes on a Turtle
3-2-1 Learn, SV 9781419099267

Friendly Frogs

Directions: Talk about how frogs hop well because they have strong hind legs. Invite your child to hop like a frog. Then have your child look at the frogs below and draw an **X** on the one that is different.

A Different Frog
3-2-1 Learn, SV 9781419099267

Hungry Fish

Directions: Invite your child to observe fish swimming in a fishbowl or aquarium. Then have your child trace the triangles to complete the fish in the picture. Invite your child to color the picture.

Triangle Fish
3-2-1 Learn, SV 9781419099267

Baby Chicks

Directions: Invite your child to observe an egg. Explain that sometimes a mother hen lays eggs that have baby chicks inside them. Have your child count the baby chicks in the picture and use a yellow crayon to color them.

Six Chicks
3-2-1 Learn, SV 9781419099267

In the Barn

Directions: Have your child compare how the tiger and the cow are alike and different. Guide your child to tell where each animal might live. Then invite your child to draw a circle around the animal that might live in a barn.

Dinnertime

Directions: Show your child a picture of a horse eating grass or hay. Talk about the kind of food that a horse eats. Invite your child to help the horse get to the barn for dinner by completing the maze.

89

A Horse Maze
3-2-1 Learn, SV 9781419099267

Long, Long Ago

Directions: Read a book about dinosaurs to your child. Choose a book with pictures of what the environment might have looked like at the time they lived. Talk about how there were volcanoes that were shaped like triangles. Have your child trace the triangle to complete the picture. Invite your child to color the picture.

Triangle Volcano
3-2-1 Learn, SV 9781419099267

Find the Footprint

Directions: Have your child make a footprint in sand. Tell your child that footprints of dinosaurs have been found and that they have given scientists clues as to how big the dinosaurs were. Invite your child to draw lines to match the dinosaurs with the footprints that are the correct size.

Sizes of Dinosaurs
3-2-1 Learn, SV 9781419099267

Teeth Need Good Care

Directions: Tell your child that teeth help make our smile pretty and that we need them for chewing. Demonstrate to your child how to brush and floss teeth properly. Invite your child to draw an **X** on the pictures that are bad for teeth and color the pictures that are good for teeth.

Kinds of Tooth Care
3-2-1 Learn, SV 9781419099267

Drawing Teeth

Directions: Have your child observe his or her teeth in the mirror. Point out that the teeth in the front of the mouth are shaped like squares. Talk about how we need our teeth to help us chew our food. Invite your child to draw four square teeth in the mouth.

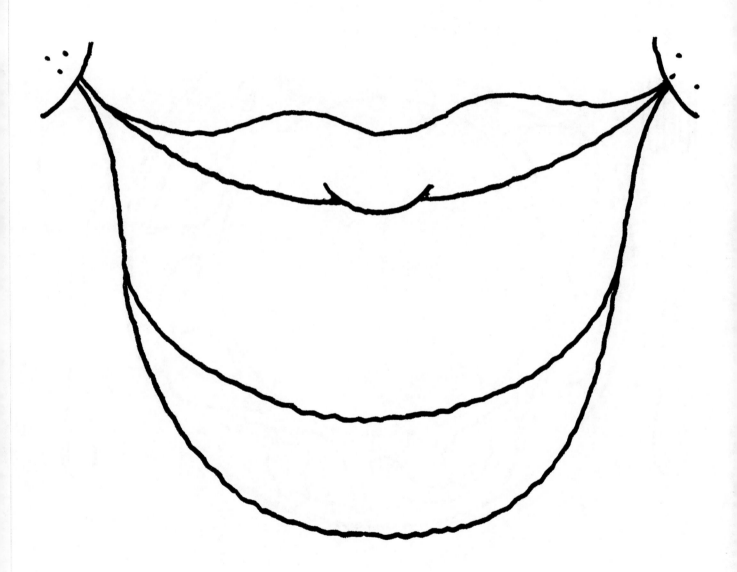

A Good Meal

Directions: Have your child name the foods on his or her plate at mealtime. Talk about how the body needs healthy foods that will help it grow. Invite your child to draw three healthy foods on the plate.

Healthy Foods
3-2-1 Learn, SV 9781419099267

Fun in the Sun

Directions: Have your child observe the sunlight coming through a window and feel the warmth of the windowpane. Talk about how the sun provides us with warmth and light so we can do many fun things outside. Have your child name the outside activities and trace the circle that shows the shape of the sun

A Circle Sun
3-2-1 Learn, SV 9781419099267

Moon Shapes

Directions: Read a book to your child about the phases of the moon, such as *Moonbear* by Frank Asch. Point out that the shape of the moon seems to change each month. Have your child draw a circle around the moons in each row that are the same.

Compare Moon Shapes
3-2-1 Learn, SV 9781419099267

Shiny Stars

Directions: Invite your child to look at the stars in the night sky and observe how some areas have more stars than others. Invite your child to circle the group of stars in each row that has more stars.

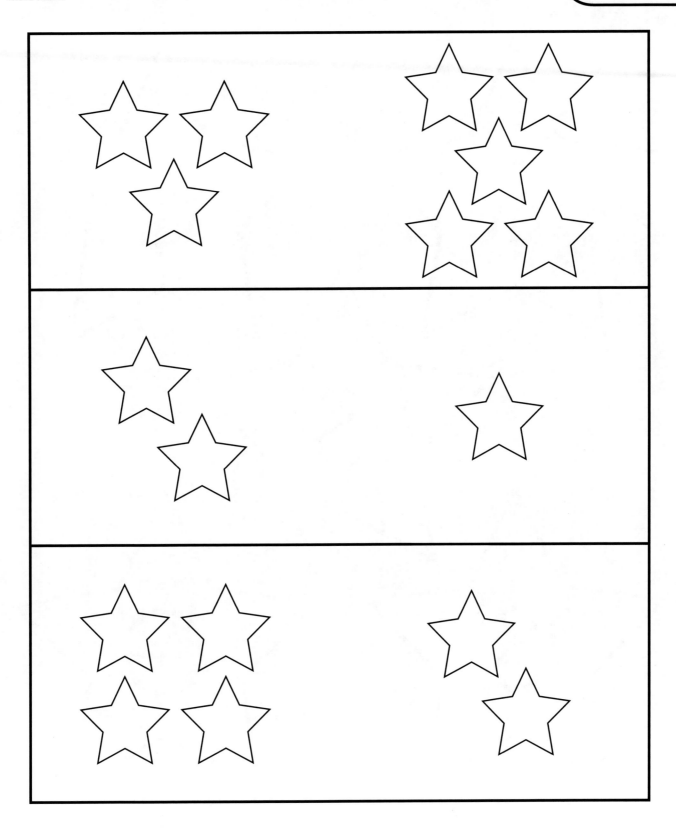

More Stars
3-2-1 Learn, SV 9781419099267

Super Stars

Directions: Tell your child that stars are different colors and sizes. Then write the word *star* and point out that it starts with the letter *s*. Have your child use a yellow crayon to color all of the stars with the letter *S*.

Match the Stars
3-2-1 Learn, SV 9781419099267

The Right Kind of Clothes

Directions: Invite your child to observe the weather for a few days. Talk about how weather is sometimes hot and sometimes cold and how we dress according to the weather. Have your child use a red crayon to color the clothes that are worn in hot weather and a blue crayon to color the clothes that are worn in cold weather.

Hot or Cold Weather
3-2-1 Learn, SV 9781419099267

Thermometers

Directions: Show your child different kinds of thermometers. Explain that we can tell how hot or cold the weather is by looking at the red part, or tube, of a thermometer. Invite your child to draw a circle around the tallest thermometer. Then have your child use a red crayon to draw a line from the bottom of each thermometer tube to the middle.

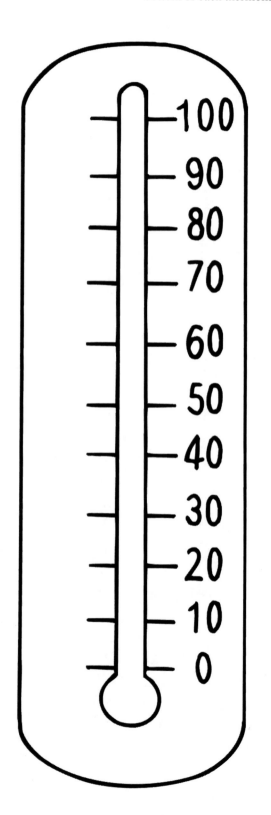

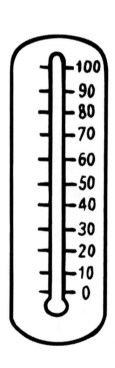

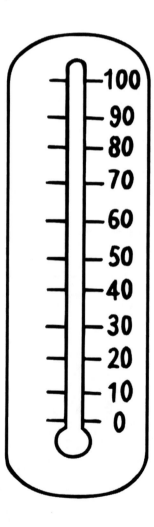

A Rainy Day

Directions: On a rainy day, invite your child to use his or her senses to see, hear, touch, smell, and taste the rain. Then have your child complete the umbrella and color the picture.

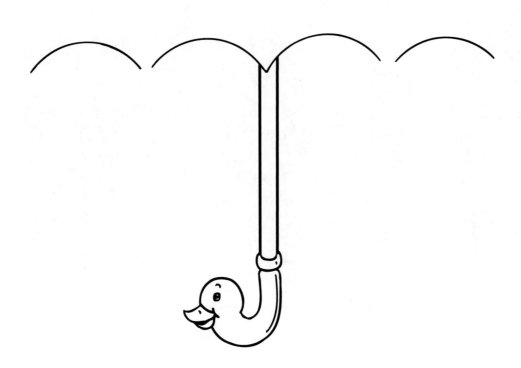

Sensing Rain
3-2-1 Learn, SV 9781419099267

Youngest and Oldest

Directions: Talk to your child about the members in your family and identify who is the oldest member and who is the youngest member. Have your child circle the oldest person in each row and draw a line under the youngest person in each row.

Compare Family Members
3-2-1 Learn, SV 9781419099267

Family Fun

Directions: Encourage your child to tell about his or her favorite outside family activity. Have your child draw a circle around and color the activities that are usually done with families while outside.

Outside Family Fun
3-2-1 Learn, SV 9781419099267

Houses Have Shapes

Directions: Invite your child to look at the houses along a street and identify the shapes of the doors, windows, and roofs. Then have your child count and color the shapes in the picture. Encourage your child to use a red crayon to color the circle, a blue crayon to color the triangles, and a green crayon to color the rectangles.

House Shapes
3-2-1 Learn, SV 9781419099267

Whose House?

Directions: Talk to your child about how people and some animals live in houses to protect them from the weather. Have your child draw lines to match the boy and the animals to their houses.

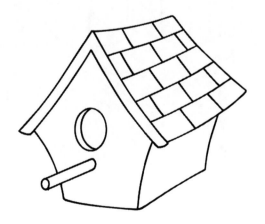

Match Their Houses
3-2-1 Learn, SV 9781419099267

A Party with Friends

Directions: Talk to your child about what happens at a birthday party. Have your child tell what is happening in the picture and what might happen next. Then have your child count the children and color the picture.

Count Friends
3-2-1 Learn, SV 9781419099267

Lots of Cakes

Directions: Take your child to the bakery section of the grocery store and observe the different kinds of cakes. Talk to your child about birthday cakes that have candles on them. Have your child color the cakes that are the same in each row.

Cakes Are the Same
3-2-1 Learn, SV 9781419099267

Happy Birthday

Directions: Tell your child that sometimes families celebrate birthdays by putting candles on a cake. Then have your child look at the picture and tell what is missing. Invite your child to draw candles to complete the picture. Have your child color the picture.

Missing Candles
3-2-1 Learn, SV 9781419099267

A Penny

Directions: Show your child the penny below. Explain that many coins have pictures of people who are presidents on them. Talk to your child about how we use money to buy things. Have your child draw a penny by tracing the circle and drawing a face on it. Invite your child to use a brown crayon to color both pennies.

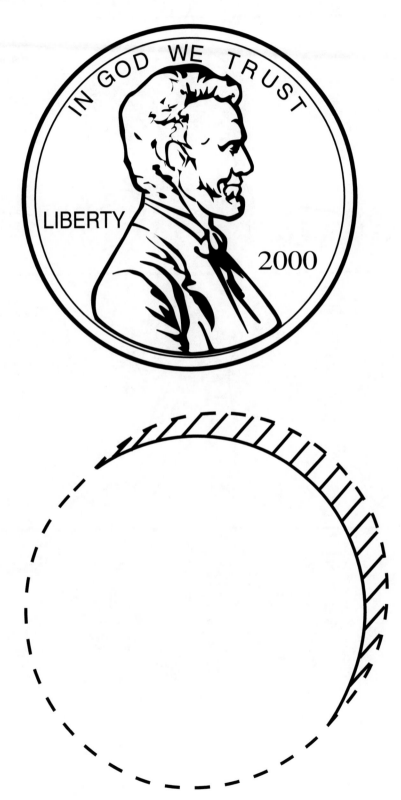

A Circle Penny
3-2-1 Learn, SV 9781419099267

Piggy Banks

Directions: Talk to your child about how people can save money to buy things they want. Have your child color the piggy bank in each row that has more pennies.

More Pennies
3-2-1 Learn, SV 9781419099267

Going to Work

Directions: Talk to your child about people who do jobs that help the community and about the special vehicles they use for their jobs. Have your child draw lines to match the workers with the correct vehicles.

Jobs People Do
3-2-1 Learn, SV 9781419099267

Lots of Mail

Directions: Have your child help take the mail out of the family's mailbox. Tell your child that a mail carrier's job is to deliver a letter to the correct mailbox. Then have your child color the envelopes that match the letter on the mailbox.

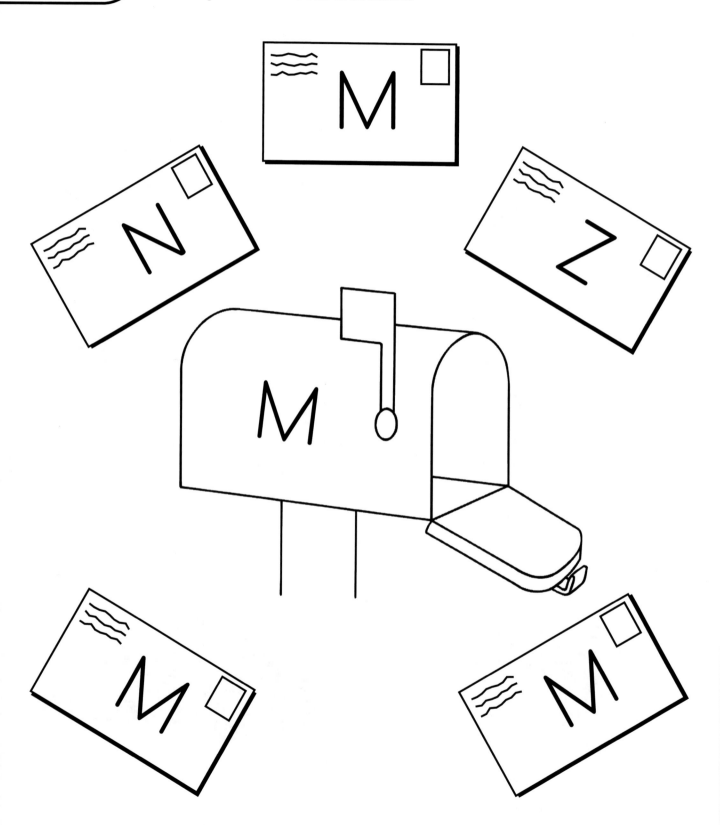

Match the Letters
3-2-1 Learn, SV 9781419099267

To the Post Office

Directions: Take a trip with your child to the neighborhood post office and point out how following the correct path helps people get to where they want to go. Then have your child draw a line from the mail truck to the post office and color the picture.

Post Office Maze
3-2-1 Learn, SV 9781419099267

See the Doctor

Directions: Have your child tell about a time he or she went to a doctor. Then have your child color the pictures that show what might happen at a doctor's office.

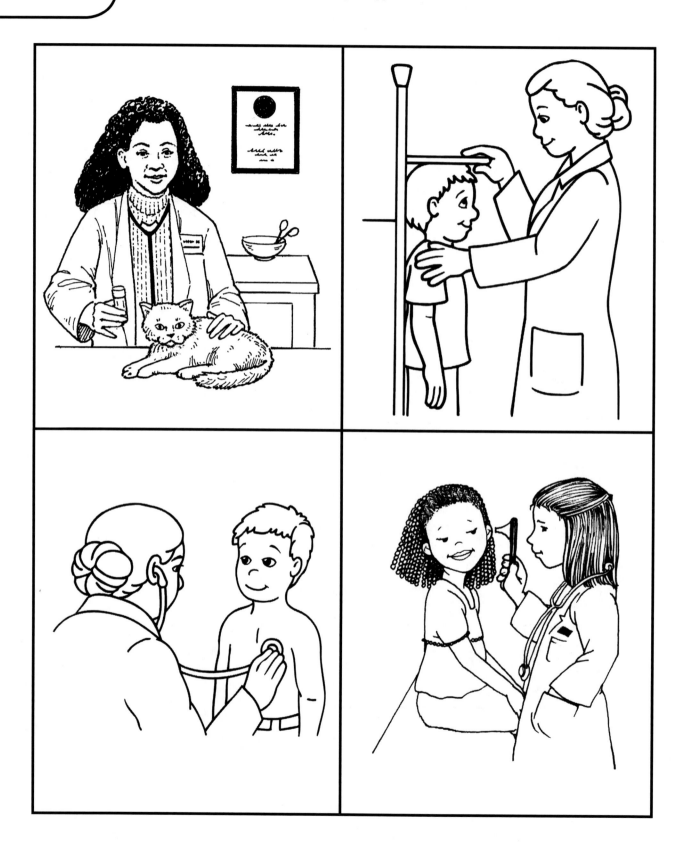

A Visit to the Doctor
3-2-1 Learn, SV 9781419099267

I Can Hammer

Directions: Show your child a hammer and some nails and talk about how they are used. Have your child sing the song below to the tune of "Here We Go 'Round the Mulberry Bush." Then have your child color the picture.

This is the way I hammer a nail,
Hammer a nail, hammer a nail.
This is the way I hammer a nail
When I build a house.

A Hammer Song
3-2-1 Learn, SV 9781419099267

Food Store

Directions: Visit a grocery store with your child and observe the variety of foods that are available. Have your child connect the dots to complete the picture. Then have your child draw in each window a food item that can be bought at a grocery store. Invite your child to color the picture.

Connect-the-Dots Grocery Store
3-2-1 Learn, SV 9781419099267

Pet Fish

Directions: Talk to your child about the responsibilities of owning a pet. Visit a pet store with your child and look at the different kinds of fish for sale. Point out that the word *fish* begins with the letter *f*. Have your child use an orange crayon to color all of the sections that have the letter *F*.

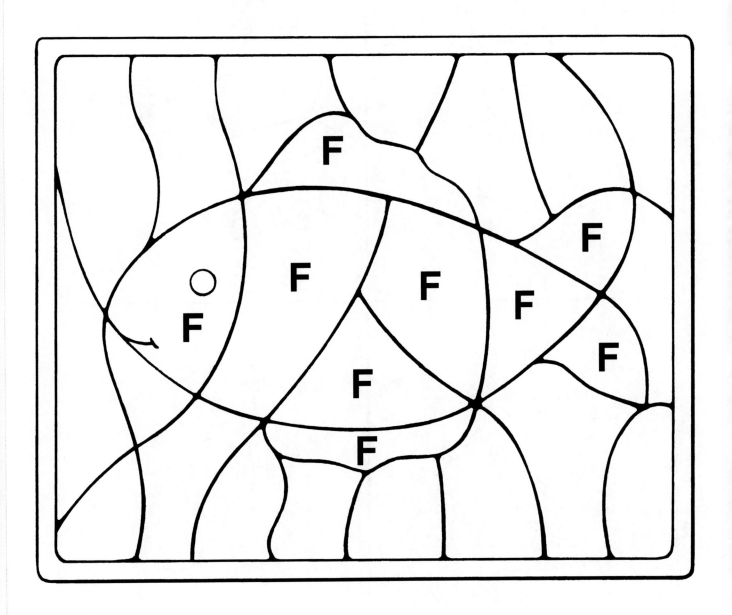

3-2-1 Learn, SV 9781419099267

Toys

Directions: Visit a toy store with your child and observe how the toys are grouped together in the aisles. Have your child count the toys in each group and circle the correct number.

Count the Toys
3-2-1 Learn, SV 9781419099267

Clowns and Balloons

Directions: Talk to your child about how clowns perform at the circus to entertain people. Have your child count all the clowns and then count all the balloons. Ask your child if there are more clowns or balloons. Then have your child color the picture.

More Clowns
3-2-1 Learn, SV 9781419099267

Funny Clowns

Directions: Talk to your child about the many different kinds of animals that work in a circus. Have your child use a brown crayon to color the animal that is being *pulled* by a clown and a gray crayon to color the animal that is being *pushed* by a clown.

Push or Pull at the Circus
3-2-1 Learn, SV 9781419099267

At the Zoo

Directions: Have your child name the kinds of animals that might be seen at a zoo. Then have your child use a brown crayon to color the animal that is on the *left* side of its cage and a black crayon to color the animal that is on the *right* side of its cage.

See the Parade

Directions: Together with your child, observe a parade or look at pictures of a parade. Talk to your child about the people in a parade who carry banners and play marching music. Have your child draw an **X** on the person who does not belong in the parade. Then have your child color the picture.

Belongs in a Parade
3-2-1 Learn, SV 9781419099267

Two Flags

Directions: Observe the design and colors on the United States flag with your child. Point out the stripes on the flag. Have your child draw the lines from left to right to complete the second flag. Encourage your child to use a white crayon, a red crayon, and a blue crayon to color the first flag. Then have your child tell how the flags are the same and different.

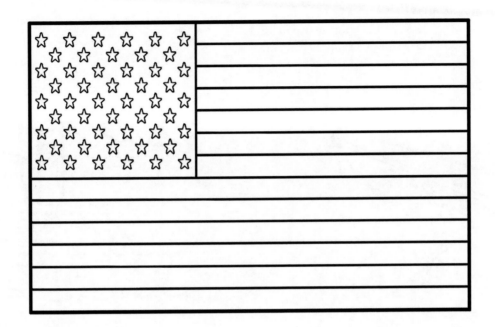

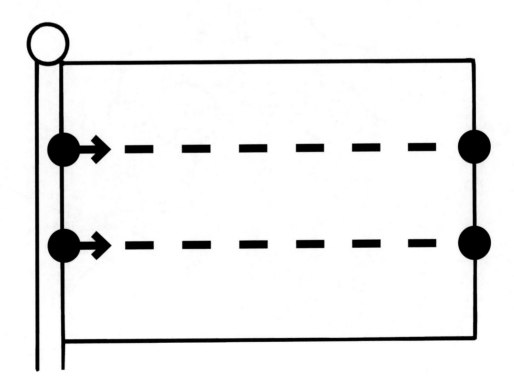

Stripes on the Flag
3-2-1 Learn, SV 9781419099267

Air, Land, or Water

Directions: Sing the song to the tune of "Twinkle, Twinkle Little Star." Have your child point to the picture of each type of transportation as it is named in the song. Then have your child use a red crayon to color the things that go in the air, a green crayon to color the things that go on land, and a blue crayon to color the things that go in the water.

Ride a car or ride a train.
Ride a boat or ride a plane.
Ride a bike or ride a bus.
These are things that transport us.
Ride a helicopter way up high.
Or ride a rocket to the sky.

A Transportation Song
3-2-1 Learn, SV 9781419099267

Red, Yellow, and Green

Directions: Observe a traffic light with your child. Explain that people can tell when it is their turn to stop or go according to the colors on the light. Tell your child the meaning of each color. Have your child use a red crayon to color the top light, a yellow crayon to color the middle light, and a green crayon to color the bottom light.

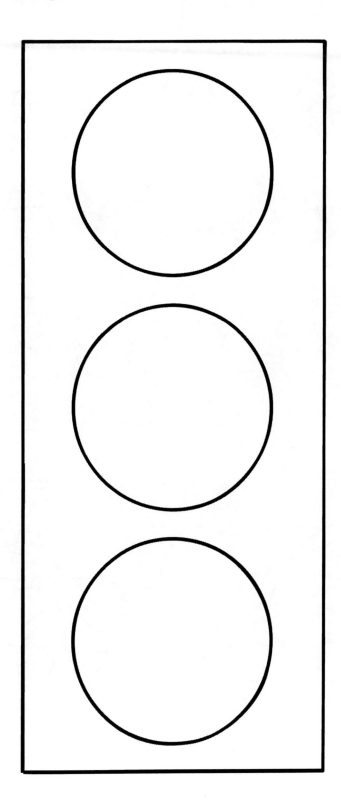

Top to Bottom Traffic Light
3-2-1 Learn, SV 9781419099267

Wheels on Cars

Directions: Tell your child that cars have wheels. Have your child color the cars whose wheels have letters that are the same.

Match the Car Wheels
3-2-1 Learn, SV 9781419099267

Two Trains

Directions: Tell your child that trains are used to take people, animals, or cargo from one place to another. Have your child use a black crayon to color the engine of the train going *over* the hill and a green crayon to color the engine that is going *under* the hill.

A Train over the Hill
3-2-1 Learn, SV 9781419099267

Two Boats

Directions: Together with your child, observe the cars that are parked on a street. Talk about how the cars that are far away look smaller than the cars that are nearer. Have your child use a brown crayon to color the boat that is *near* and an orange crayon to color the boat that is *far away*.

Boats Near and Far
3-2-1 Learn, SV 9781419099267